Riley &
Janie Mitchell

Riley & Janie Mitchell

A Proud & Lasting Legacy of Family, Faith, Love & Courage

ERIC A. MITCHELL

To order additional copies of this book, contact:
Xlibris Corporation
1-888-795-4274
www.Xlibris.com
Orders@Xlibris.com
116649

CONTENTS

Eric Mitchell & Family

In dedication to my Dad, Jerry Mitchell.
For the unconditional love, sacrifice
and life lessons given to our family.
For imparting to me the ongoing desire
to remember and appreciate our
family and their many accomplishments.

ACKNOWLEDGEMENTS

I would like to thank all of my family for supporting this effort to memorialize our proud past & acknowledge that history is continually being made. As is said, "We must know where we come from in order to know where we are going."

Special thanks to Aunt Mary Jane and Aunt Georgia for providing their DNA sample to make our African connection even possible and for remembering and sharing their memories of our incredible family. Rest in Peace!

Photos of Riley and Janie Mitchell

RILEY & JANIE MITCHELL-LIFE FULFILLED

This is the story of Riley ("Papa") & Janie ("Sus") Mitchell. They both built a foundation of love, ambition, faith and charity in Koenton, Alabama, a small rural section of Washington County. Upon this foundation, they imparted these attributes to their family that would serve to sustain and continue their legacy for generations to come. Their strength and courage, especially in the face of adversity and discrimination, would forever serve as a shining example and invaluable lesson for living. By any measure, they lived a life full of accomplishment and excellence. This Book is just a small attempt to highlight a few of their many accomplishments and sacrifice. Through acknowledging and remembering them, we are also empowered and can unlock those same attributes to assist us with fulfilling our purpose-driven lives.

"Bringing the gifts that my ancestors gave, I am the dream and the hope of the slave. I Rise, I Rise, I Rise"-Maya Angelou

In 1875, Riley was born to the union of Issac and Lucy Mitchell. On January 26, 1876, Janie was born to the union of Will and Georgiana Jackson. Both Riley and Janie would later be married in Koenton, Alabama and were blessed with 14 children. Their children were:

Willie ("Big Daddy");   Mile ("Preacher");

Julius;   John ("Tit");

Riley ("Bo Leg");   Isaac;

Eva;   Lucille ("Lucy");

Woodrow ("Duster");   Sears ("Buster");

Jonas;   Georgia;

Charlie;   Mary Jane.

They were blessed with even more grandchildren. In the year 2012, it is estimated that Riley and Janie's direct descendants would span over eight generations, comprising almost two thousand family members.

Owning land and providing for their family and the larger Koenton community from the fruits of their labor, was very important to Riley (Papa) and Janie (Sus). It was Sus that often encouraged Papa to continue to purchase more land. At the time of Papa Riley's death in 1950, it was published that, "he owned more land than any other black man in Washington County." Papa Riley would eventually own a 'section' of land, equal to 648 acres, plus an additional 40 acres. This land was farmed by Papa, Sus, their family and many residents throughout the Koenton community. They were able to produce their own food, clothing and goods. Cotton and corn were two of the many crops that were harvested on their land. They also produced syrup from their own sugarcane mill. They had their own sawmill to cut timber. It was said that at one time, Papa and Sus had approximately 30 calves and 7 plow horses. They often traded with other families in the Koenton community or sold goods to others outside their community. Their hard work and ownership of the land allowed the Koenton community to be self-sufficient and protected from other racially hostile communities in Alabama at that time.

"The nation that destroys it's soil destroys itself"-Pres. Franklin Roosevelt

Their generosity to others within the Koenton community also allowed the community to continue to grow and thrive. Papa and Sus gave parcels of their land to both family and non-family members and built dozens of homes for others. Their generosity was also seen when community members would come to their land with tin pales to collect milk or when a newly married couple in the community would be gifted a Calf to assist with starting their own lives.

Papa and Sus recognized the importance for their children and other children in Koenton to have access to a quality education. They would eventually help support several of their children through College. In 1919, they donated 2 acres of land for the construction of the Koenton Rosenwald Junior High School that would serve grades 1-9. This white-framed structure sat atop a hill and initially comprised two classrooms and a principal's office. Both Papa and Sus served as founding members of the school and their daughter, Georgia (Butler) Mitchell would serve as its' first Principal from 1919 until 1921, after attending Selma College. In 1938, Papa and Sus would donate 3 additional acres for the school to be expanded and re-designated as the Koenton High School. It would then serve grades 1-12.
As a result of their generosity, the school was enlarged throughout several buildings and comprised 5 classrooms, a lunchroom, a snack shop, a multi-purpose room for viewing movies and a teacher's dormitory. Each classroom was heated with a pot-bellied wood-burning stove. There was also a spring for water about three-fourths down the road. The school colors were maroon and gold and the mascot was the "Koenton Tigers". Although the school structures are no longer standing, there is a beautiful placard at the site to commemorate this incredible accomplishment.

Papa Riley also purchased a school bus to transport children to school. That bus was utilized to service the community by transporting them to Church, games and other places. Papa Riley was also instrumental in building a school in a nearby community.

> *"Children learn more from what you are than what you teach"*-W.E.B. DuBois

Both Papa and Sus were also Christians and religion played a major role in their lives and was an influential factor in the upbringing of their 14 children. In 1949 and 1950, they donated land, organized and eventually constructed the New True Light Baptist Church in the Koenton community so that Koenton residents would have a safe place to worship. Papa Riley served as Chairman of its' first Deacon Board. Papa Riley also took steps to set aside land adjacent to the Church for purposes of providing and maintaining a community cemetery. New True Light Baptist Church continues to serve the community today and the cemetery remains available to local residents without charge.

"God can do anything but fail"-African-American Proverb

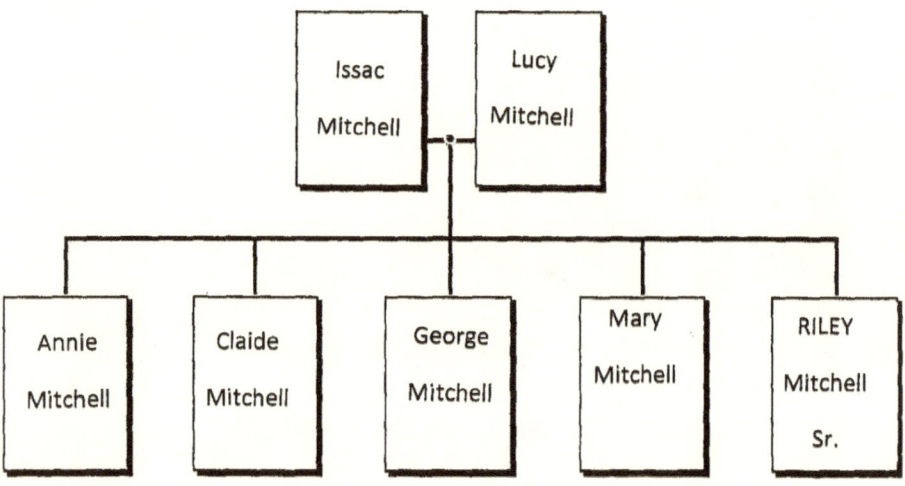

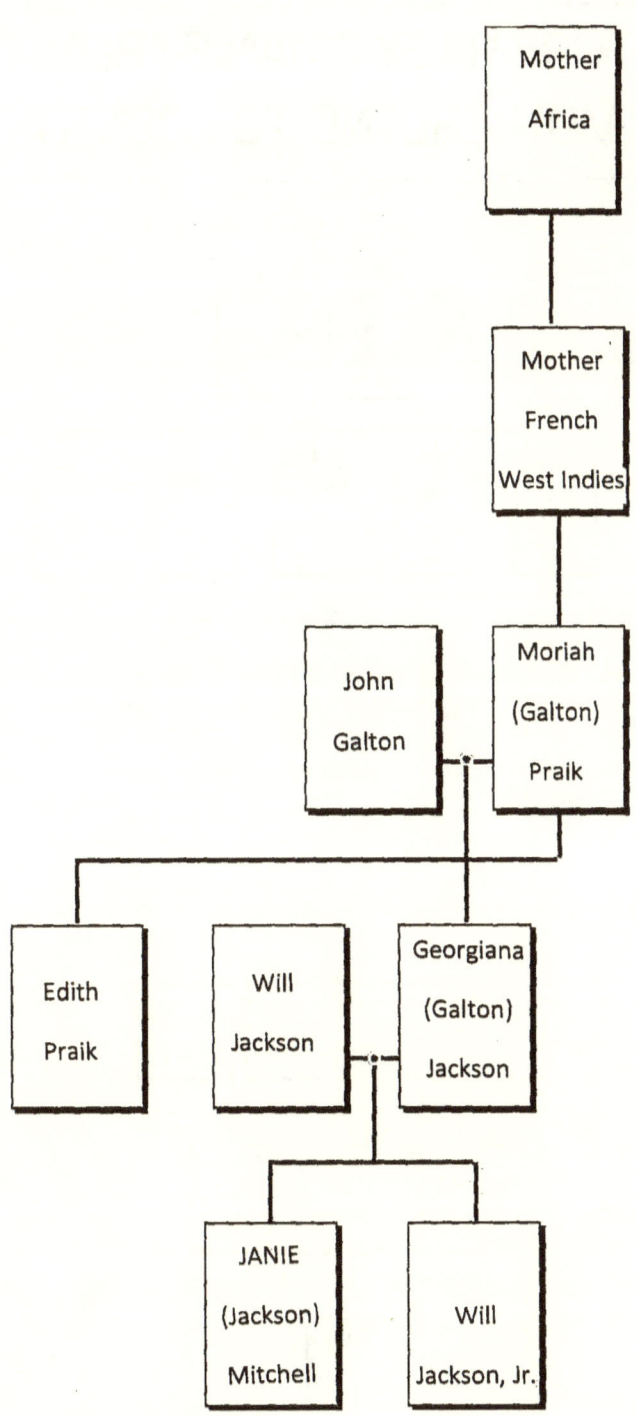

BEFORE RILEY & JANIE-FROM THE MOTHERLAND TO KOENTON

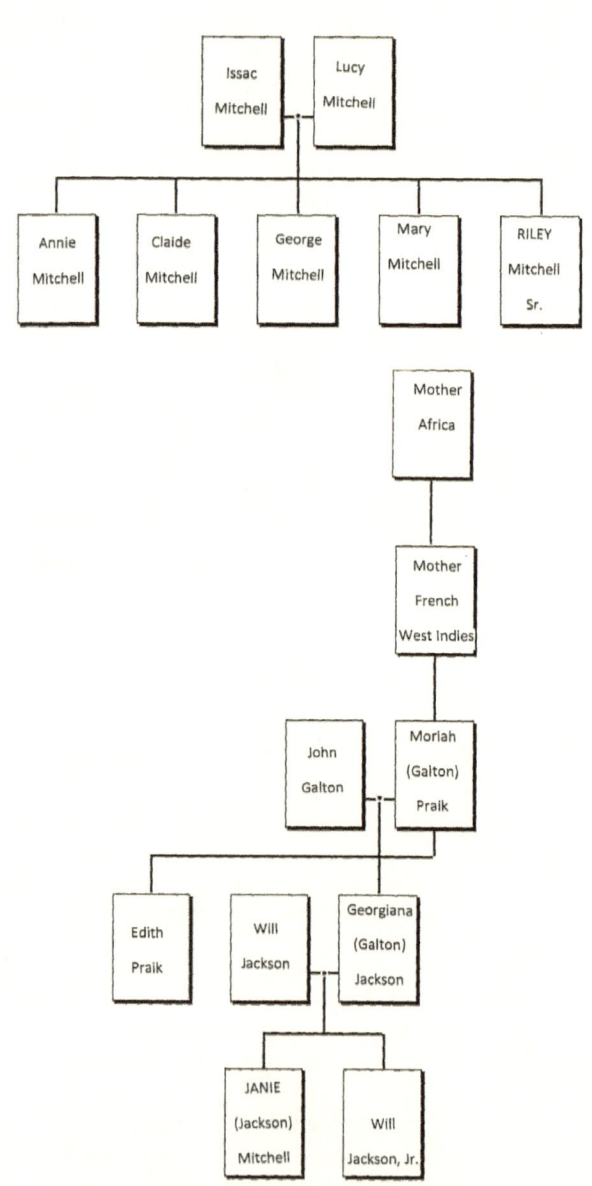

As a result of mitochondrial DNA samples provided by Mary Jane Washington and Georgia Butler in 2010, experts have determined that our most recent female African ancestor originated from a region that comprises modern-day Angola & the Republic of Congo. Throughout history, Africans along the western coast of Angola and the Republic of Congo have been made up of strong and proud Bantu tribes. Some of these tribes would include Vili, Kongo, Teke and Kimbundu. They have also made a living by fishing, hunting, working the soil and being skilled craftsmen. Both Angola and the Republic of Congo are rich in iron, copper, gold, diamonds and oil. These resources have madethese two countries potentially some of the wealthiest in the World. Before slavery came to Africa, our ancestors were Kings and Queens and lived off a rich and plentiful land while exercising their African traditions and culture.

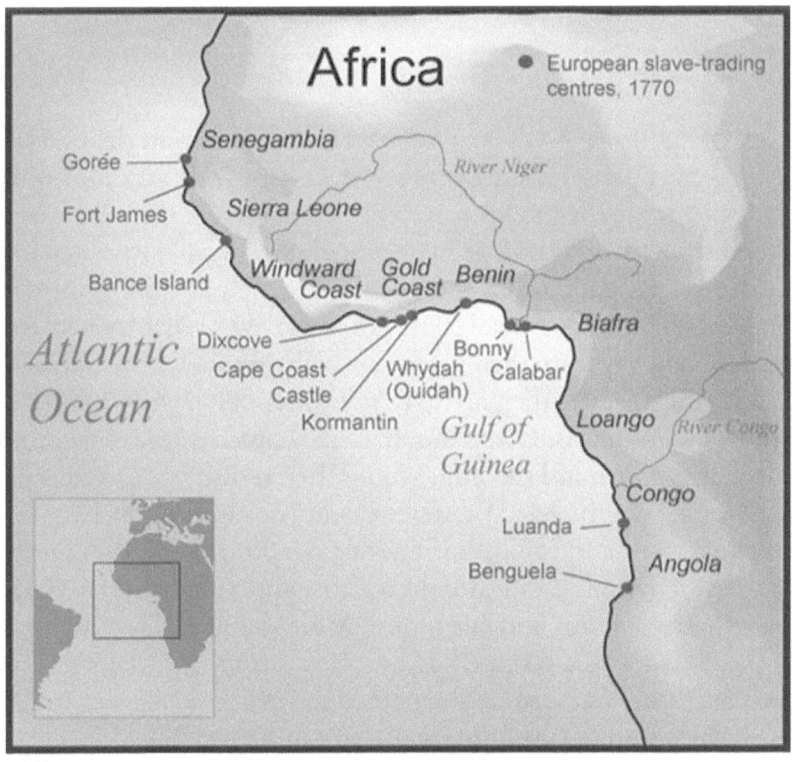

As a result of slavery, our African ancestors were taken from their homes and experienced great pain and suffering, but their survival is a testimony to their strength and courage. With knowing the obstacles that they overcame, this allows their strength and courage to be passed down to all future generations. The Atlantic slave trade was a form of triangular trade. Slave ships would leave France and other European countries and arrive in Africa where Africans were kidnapped away from their homes and sold into bondage and servitude. The packed ships would then arrive in the Americas or the Caribbean after sailing for 1 to 6 months. Often the Africans would be traded for molasses, rum or other supplies and the ships would then return back to Europe. The Africans would then be left in different countries in the Americas and the Caribbean to work and toil in horrendous conditions and do their best to survive. Over a period of four hundred years, approximately 15-20 million Africans experienced this horrible ordeal. More than 4 million Africans died during this journey as a result of disease, starvation, and the length of the passage. This experience is sometimes called the Maafa by African Americans. This term means holocaust or great disaster in KiSwahili.

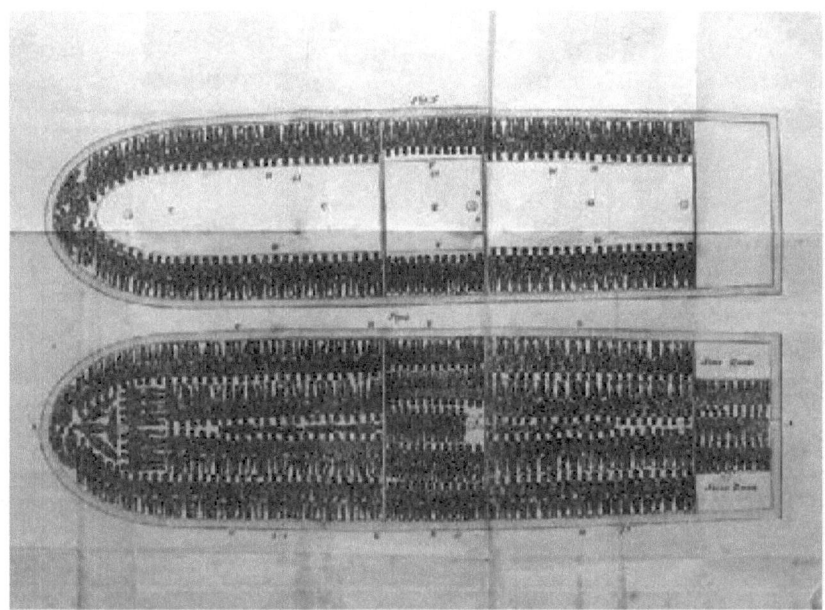

Based upon DNA results, extensive research and oral accounts that have been passed down through the generations, our "Mother Africa", would have been the great-grandmother of Georgiana Jackson. "Mother Africa" was forcibly removed from Africa into Slavery at the French Slave Port of Loango, Congo. This Port is just North of Pointe Noire, Congo. It is estimated that during the slave trade, approximately 2 million Africans left from this Loango Port. In 2012, the local tribal leaders allowed our Mitchell Family to leave a granite marker at the site of this former slave port in tribute and remembrance of our ancestor, "Mother Africa". The marker reads as follows: "Mother Africa"—You were taken from this land centuries ago and now we, your descendants, flourish and are numbered in the thousands. Thank God for your Strength, Perseverance & Love. In Love and Spirit, Your Mitchell Family, Koenton, Alabama, U.S.A., March 27, 2012.

From the year 1626 to 1850, the French would remove 1.4 million Africans to the islands of the French West Indies in over 4000 voyages. Our "Mother Africa" was likely transported to the French West Indian Islands of Martinique or Guadeloupe on a French slave ship in the late 1700's to work and toil on a sugar plantation. "Mother Africa" would eventually give birth to her daughter, ("Mother French West Indies"). In approximately 1832, "Mother French West Indies" gave birth to her daughter named Moriah. The name "Moriah" in French means dark-skinned girl. Moriah was remembered to have a dark complexion with long beautiful hair and she also spoke the French language. During the 1830's, the institution of slavery began to sharply decline in the French West Indies, as a result of a drop in

World wide sugar prices, which made the sugar plantations less profitable and from the efforts of French Abolitionists, such Victor Schoelcher and others, who raised awareness to the injustices associated with Slavery.

As a result of these changes, "Mother French West Indies" and her daughter "Moriah" were together placed on a French slave ship in 1838 to be transported to the United States to be sold as slaves. Around 1838, Moriah and her mother arrived in the Port of Charleston, South Carolina. Moriah was 6 years old when she arrived in the United States with her Mother. After unboarding the Slave ship, Moriah and "Mother French West Indies" were separated and both sold into slavery at a slave auction. Moriah would never see her Mother again.

From 1838 until the end of the Civil War in 1865, Moriah was enslaved and worked in the fields of a South Carolina Plantation. In 1850, Moriah gave birth to a girl, who she would name Georgiana. Georgiana was bi-racial. Georgiana's father was the slave holder, John Galton. While Moriah worked in the fields, Georgiana worked as a Slave in the plantation home. She often lit her Father's smoking pipe. After working in the fields, Moriah would come to the slave house and Georgiana and her would talk to each other through a side window. Georgiana would also give her Mother bread made from corn scraps. When Slavery ended at the end of the Civil war in 1865, Georgiana was 15 years old. Both Moriah and Georgiana were informed by the slaveholding family that they both could stay on the Plantation. They both decided to leave together and chart out a new course for their lives. Moriah (Galton) Praik would eventually marry and have another daughter, named Edith.

"Freedom is never given; it is won"-A. Philip Randolph

Photo of Georgiana Jackson

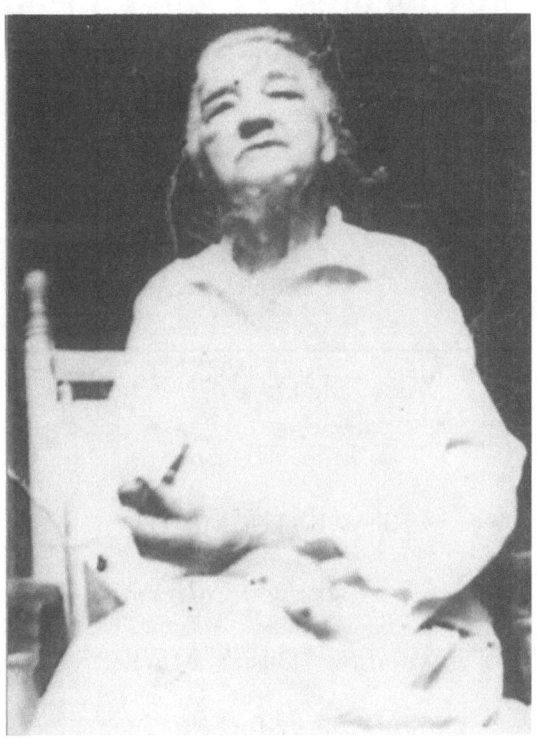

After Slavery ended, Georgiana still experienced many challenges. She had little money and resources. Before arriving in Koenton (Washington County) Alabama, it is anticipated that she lived in several towns trying to make a life for herself. For a period of time, she resided in Bladon Springs, Alabama, which is in Choctaw County. In Koenton, Alabama, Georgiana would marry Will Jackson and they would raise two children, Will, Jr. and Janie. Georgiana held the distinction of being a trained midwife. For decades, she delivered many babies for both Black and White families throughout Koenton and Washington County. She was remembered for smoking a pipe. She continued to serve as a pillar of support and inspiration for the Koenton community until her death on February 24, 1950.

A CONTINUING FAMILY LEGACY

Riley & Janie Mitchell
(14 children)

Willie "Big Daddy" Mitchell

Julius Mitchell

Riley "Bo Leg" Mitchell

Eva (Mitchell) Coleman

Woodrow "Duster" Mitchell

Jonas Mitchell

Charlie Mitchell

Mile "Preacher" Mitchell

John "Tit" Mitchell

Issac Mitchell

Lucille (Mitchell) Blackmon

Sears "Buster" Mitchell

Georgia (Mitchell) Butler

Mary Jane (Mitchell) Washington

The legacy of sacrifice, courage and achievement that Papa Riley and Sus left their family continues to this very day. The descendants of Papa and Sus have excelled in every field of human endeavor, including but not limited to the fields of: education, business, law, medicine, law enforcement, Theology, professional athletics and philanthropy. The Mitchell family will continue to learn from past and present lessons as they steer a course for an even brighter future.

Woodrow "Duster" Mitchell
(no children)

Mary Jane Washington
(no children)
Husband-Frank

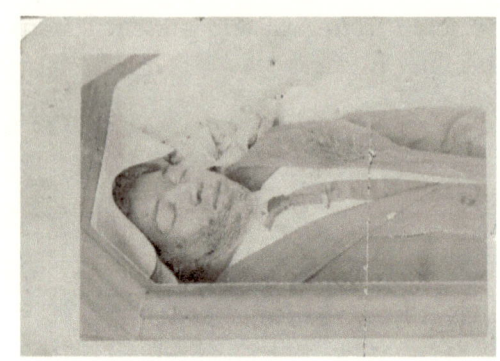

Mile "Preacher" Mitchell
(no children)

Riley "Bo Leg" Mitchell, Jr.
(2 children)
Wife-Juanita ("Drussie")

Billy Madison
Barbara Gene Mitchell

Georgia (Mitchell) Butler
(3 children)
Husband-Wade

Genevie Butler
(all 3 children passed away
at early age)

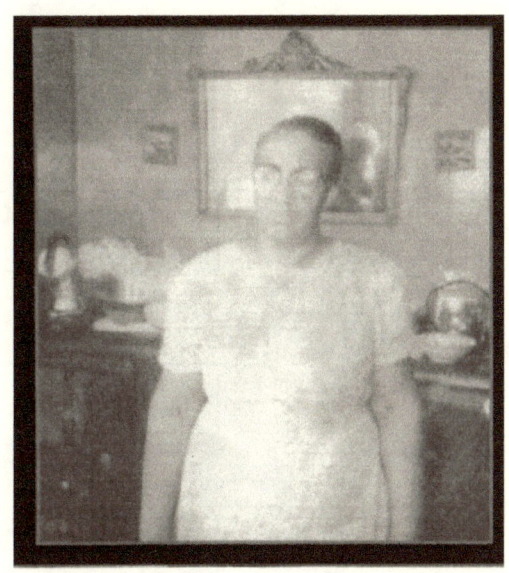

Issac Mitchell
(5 children)
Wife—Lizzy

Genevie Mitchell
O.B. Mitchell
Voncille Leverett

Eva (Mitchell) Coleman
(1 child)

Janie "Cuddie" Warren

Sears "Buster" Mitchell
(6 children)
Relationship-Fannie

McCary Mitchell

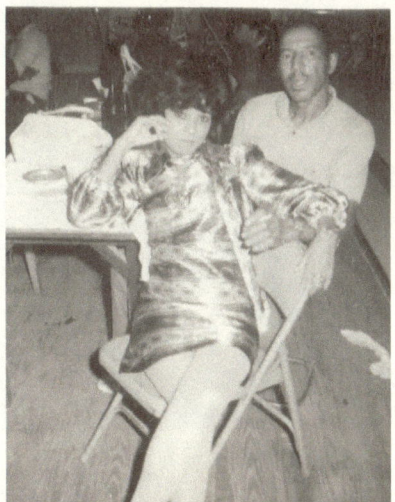

(McCary is 2nd from left)

Lucille "Lucy" Blackmon
(1 child)
Husbands=Leverett/Blackmon

Dorothy "Dot" Mitchell

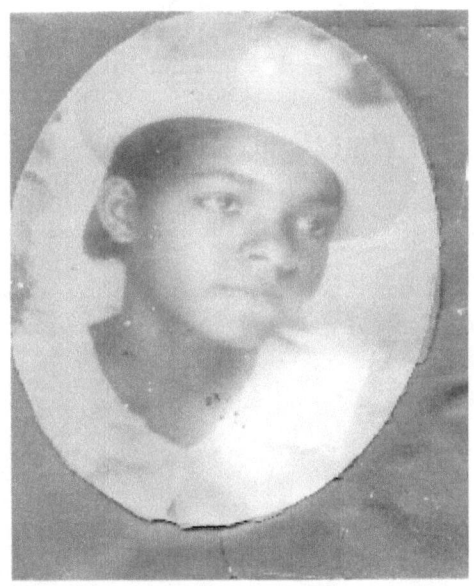

Willie "Big Daddy" Mitchell
(6 children)
Wife-Willie Bee

Bessie Mitchell

Boyd Mitchell

Charlie Mitchell

Dan Mitchell

Milton Mitchell

M.L. Mitchell

2006

ANNIE MITCHELL
(Grandmother)

THE LATE MILTON MITCHELL
(Grandfather)

John "Tit" Mitchell
(8 children)
Wife-Evangeline ("Lil Sis")

Bernice Barber

Edward "Spooky" O'Neal

Elease "Sugar Babe" Creal

John "Nook" Mitchell, Jr.

Robert "Scooney" Mitchell

Samuel Mitchell

Shirley Mitchell

Charlie Mitchell
(9 children)
Wife-Ruth

Bertha "Sis" Washington

Charles "Bud/Sleepy" Mitchell

Dolly Myers

Edith Mae Lyles

Janie Pearl Stephens

Jerry "BabyRuth" Mitchell

Ollie Johnson

Ozzie "Mane" Mitchell

Riley "Gold" Mitchell

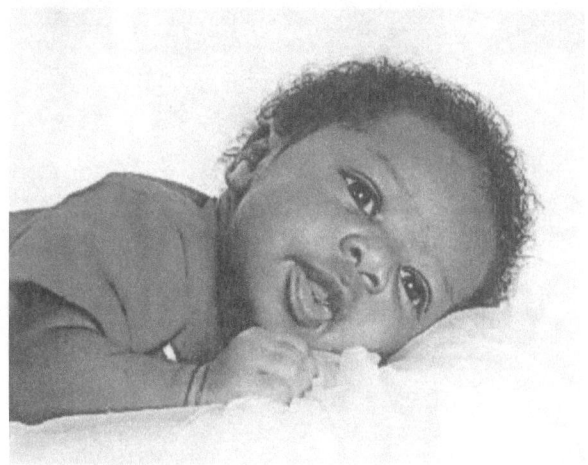

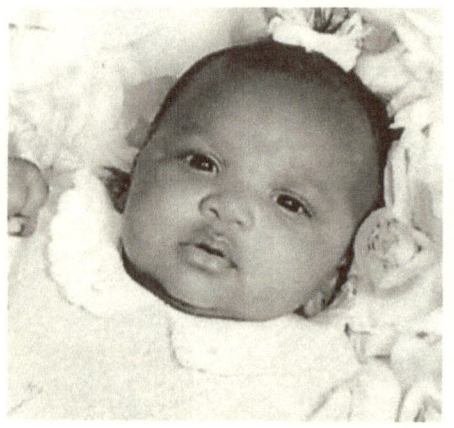

Jonas Mitchell
(12 children)
Wife-Ora

Archie "Lil Bo" Mitchell

Arthur Mitchell

Arlene "Little Sister' Turner

Florida Lindell

Jetson "Big Bud" Mitchell

John Mitchell

Jonas Mitchell, Jr.

Miles Mitchell

O.D. "Butterboy" Mitchell

Ruby Pearl Davis

Tommy Lee "Lil T" Mitchell

Queen Johnson

Julius Mitchell
(11 children)
Wife-Bessie

Aslean "*Lo*" Thomas-Norfleet

Earnest Lee Mitchell

Eugene Mitchell

Georgia Jackson

Jessie Mitchell

Joe Mitchell

Julius Mitchell, Jr.

Leroy Mitchell

Marvin Mitchell

Rose Crisler

Vincie Youngblood

PASSED DOWN FAMILY STORY-TELLING

During Slavery

*Moriah was beaten when her daughter, Georgiana was delivered because Georgiana was bi-racial.

*Papa Riley's Mother, Lucy, was short with a dark complexion. She often cooked peas and fatback in a pot. She liked to smoke and dance the "huck a buck". She had a garden and loved to eat meat that Riley would often buy for her. She died at the age of 112.

*Grandma Georgiana also had 2 brothers with straight hair that came down with fever and they were left on the side of the road to die by the slaveholder.

After Slavery

*Grandma Georgiana and her sister, Edith would go to parties together in Mississippi.

*The Jim Crow era was a very difficult period for Blacks and Aunt Mary Jane Washington referred to it as the 2nd Slavery.

*With Janie's encouragement, Papa Riley bought his first acre of land for 50 cents.

*In the early 1900's, there was only 2 to 3 months of schooling because of the necessity of children working in the fields. Georgia Butler had a bucket and 1 dipper that all those working the field would drink water from.

ADDITIONAL RESEARCH
WITH DNA RESULTS

*Based on research, this author does not believe that John Galton, slaveholder and Georgiana's Father is the same John Galton (from England) that is 18th in line from King Edward the 1st & 17th in line from Robert the Bruce.

*The last name of our ancestor, John Galton may also be Dalton or Gaulden. The source for John Galton being Georgiana's father is the Alabama death certificate of Grandma Georgiana (FHL Film # 1908867).

*It was long held that the entry point for the slave ship carrying Moriah and her Mother was Mobile, Alabama. Consequently, it was also believed that Moriah's daughter, Georgiana was also born in Alabama. The 1880 and 1920 U.S. Census also indicate that Georgiana's place of birth was Alabama. Thorough research has now deduced that Alabama is not the correct State for both of these assumptions. The actual State was South Carolina and this is based on South Carolina continuing to be the dominate slave entry port during this point in time. More importantly, Grandma Georgiana revealed in her later years of life that her actual birth State was South Carolina and not Alabama. This is reflected in the U.S. Census of 1930 and 1940, which was also confirmed by her daughter, Janie.

*Grandma Georgiana's death certificate, census entries and tombstone all have different spellings for her first name. Her death certificate has her passing away in 1952 and her tombstone says 1950. Her actual date of death was February 24, 1950.

*The DNA results place our African linkage to an area that comprises modern-day Angola and the Republic of Congo. It has been deduced that Loango, Congo was the likely departure point for "Mother Africa" because it was solely controlled by the French and our family has significant French ties. For example, "Moriah" is a French word meaning dark-skinned girl. Also, Moriah spoke French when she arrived in the United States. Finally, the DNA results reveal an ethnic composition of 68.50% West African and 31.50% French European. The 3 main slave ports in Angola, on the otherhand, were controlled by the Portuguese.

My African DNA - mtDNA Results

Position		
16129	G	A
16183	A	C
16189	T	C
16215	A	G
16223	C	T
16278	C	T
16294	C	T
16311	T	C
16360	C	T
16519	T	C

Position		
73	A	G
151	C	T
152	T	C
182	C	T
186	C	A
189	A	C
247	G	A
263	A	G
315.1		C
316	G	A
522	C	-
523	A	-

Position		
750	A	G
769	G	A
825	T	A
1018	G	A
1119	T	C
1438	A	G
2395	A	-
2706	A	G
2758	G	A
2885	T	C
3594	C	T
3666	G	A
4104	A	G
4769	A	G
5951	A	G
6071	T	C
6221	T	A
6260	G	A
6917	G	A
7028	C	T
7146	A	G
7256	C	T
7389	T	C

AUTHOR'S LINEAGE

I will forever be the Proud great-grandson of Riley & Janie Mitchell

Proud grandson of Charlie & Ruth Mitchell

Proud son of Jerry & Zandra Mitchell

Proud brother of Rolonda &Jason Mitchell

Proud husband of Daleta Mitchell

Proud father of Jade &Camryn Mitchell and;

*Proud cousin and nephew to so many. *